DREAM INTERPRETATION

DREAM

INTERPRETATION

A NEW APPROACH

THOMAS M. FRENCH

AND

ERIKA FROMM

———

———

BASIC BOOKS, INC.

PUBLISHERS

NEW YORK / LONDON

CONTENTS

Part 1: EVEN THE THOUGHT PROCESSES IN DREAMS MAKE SENSE

CHAPTER

Part 2: AN OPERATIONAL APPROACH TO INTERPRETATION AND THEORY

Part 3: PSYCHOLOGY OF DREAMING

Part 4: SUMMARY

ACKNOWLEDGMENTS

We wish to express our grateful appreciation to Dr. David Hamburg for permission to use his notes and dream material on a case which he treated with unusual sensitivity and tact.

We are also indebted to Dr. Edoardo Weiss, Dr. Philip F. D. Seitz, and Dr. Fred P. Robbins for carefully reading our manuscript and for their many helpful suggestions.

Dr. Weiss, whose own work on ego psychology has been closely related to ours, contributed important theoretical comments and helped us find the technical terms in which some of our ideas could be best expressed. Dr. Seitz's criticisms were particularly valuable in stimulating us to reorganize our discussion of the relations between our own concepts of dream psychology and those of Freud.

PART 1

EVEN THE THOUGHT PROCESSES IN DREAMS MAKE SENSE

CHECKING INTERPRETATIONS

Psychoanalytic interpretation is an intuitive art. As such, it is an essential part of the therapeutic art of any psychoanalyst who has adequate intuitive gifts and sufficient training.

We usually make no claim for psychoanalytic interpretation as a rigorous scientific procedure. Psychoanalytic interpretations are difficult to check. The purpose of the following essays is to outline systematic methods of checking our intuitive art in order to make it an adequate tool for scientific investigation. The authors' plan is to discuss the problems and principles involved when we try to develop a trustworthy method of interpretation, that is, one that can be checked systematically against all available evidence and one that yields conclusions of which we can be reasonably sure.

IS A CRITICALLY OBJECTIVE
INTERPRETIVE METHOD POSSIBLE?

We are certain that many psychoanalysts will view this venture of ours with some skepticism. Freud (1912) described the interpretive process as follows: The analyst, Freud said, must turn his unconscious like a receptive organ towards the transmitting unconscious of the patient. He must adjust himself to the patient as a telephone receiver is adjusted to the receiving microphone. Just as the receiver converts back into sound waves the electric oscillations in the telephone line which were set up by sound waves, so is the doctor's unconscious able—to reconstruct [the patient's] unconscious.

Freud had good reason for distrusting interpretations based on conscious logical reasoning. The thought processes required for understanding another person's unconscious are very different from those involved in scientific formulation and reasoning. Consequently, psychoanalysts often fear conscious attempts to check interpretations. They fear that conscious weighing of evidence will inhibit and distort the analyst's capacity for using his own unconscious as a tool. The authors of these essays agree that such misgivings should not be dismissed lightly.

Yet we are even more reluctant to accept the conclusion that psychoanalytic interpretations cannot be checked. We wish to show that it is possible for an analyst to learn to be objectively critical of his interpretations without disturbing the sensitive empathic resonance on which his understanding of the patient depends.

The thought processes on which intuitive interpretations are based differ from conscious reasoning in that they are neither conscious nor verbal. Their nonverbal character probably explains a seemingly paradoxical fact. Our intuitive understanding of a patient's emotional responses is superior to anything that conscious logical reasoning might reveal. This is because the mental processes that we are trying to understand are themselves nonverbal. The verbal logic that we idealize as "scientific" is another language, one with an entirely different structure.

We cannot really understand a foreign language * by translating it literally, word for word, into English. We must first catch the spirit of the language, so that we can understand the foreign text directly. Translation is an even more difficult art than understanding. Each language has its own characteristic structure; what one has learned directly in one language cannot easily be expressed in another language that has an entirely different structure. Such translation is a task that can be achieved only by a sensitive and skilled artist.

This brings us back to Freud's analogy. We understand our patients' nonverbal mental processes directly, as we do another language, by a kind of resonance. Now we ask: After the analyst's unconscious has understood the patient's unconscious by direct resonance, how do we know whether the analyst has "understood" correctly? After all, intuitive understanding may be erroneous. It is often distorted by some emotional bias of the interpreting analyst. Such a bias can be corrected only if the interpreting analyst can discover it.

Fortunately, not all errors are due to bias. Even if little or no bias has been present, it is also possible that our direct intuitive impressions have not taken account of all the available evidence or that they have not reasoned correctly from the evidence. We wish to show how it is possible to check our intuitive impressions against evidence.

Principle of Proposed Method.   A number of investigators have tried to study the interpretive process by getting the ana-

---

* Perhaps we should say "Chinese," which is the name by which our patients' unconscious symbolism often refers to the "language" of the unconscious.

lyst to report any fantasies of his own that may emerge into consciousness while he is listening to his patient. This procedure is of very little value for our present purpose. Suppose an analyst's own fantasy does suggest a particular interpretation. How is he to know whether his own fantasies accurately reflect something in the patient's unconscious? To answer this question, he must examine the evidence.

The procedure which we now propose is simple in principle, sometimes difficult in practice. The principle * is to formulate explicitly and examine conscientiously the evidence for and against our intuitive insights.

When we try to be objectively critical of our empathic "understanding," we approach the task of interpretation alternately in two ways. Both approaches are intuitive. We first use intuition imaginatively in a search for promising hypotheses, just as we would do in any intuitive method; but then we use our intuition critically in order to appraise and evaluate the products of our intuitive imagination. Our initial imaginative impression may have been based on only part of the evidence. If so, we check whether the rest of the evidence supports our interpretation. In another case, our initial intuitive understanding may even be in conflict with some of the evidence. If so, we must revise our first interpretation or even look for a better one to replace it.

* This procedure is, of course, not really new. Actually, most intuitive analysts integrate imagination and critical judgment preconsciously in their interpretations. Especially for purposes of scientific investigation, however, critical scrutiny can be more thorough and adequate when the imaginative and critical parts of the interpretive process can be disentangled and performed as two separate intuitive acts. Lawrence S. Kubie (1952, 1953) has, in fact, proposed that interpretations be regarded as hypotheses to be tested. T. M. French has also twice previously (1944, 1952) spelled out the advantages of separating imagination and critical scrutiny in the interpretive process.

There is a widespread impression, even among psychoanalysts, that the actual thought processes in dreams are strange and incomprehensible. This impression, which has been encouraged by Freud's first description of the "primary process," is one of the chief obstacles to a really critical approach to dream interpretation. The opposite assumption is a much better guide, if we are earnest in our purpose to understand what the dreamer was really thinking about. Our best working assumption is that the dreamer's thoughts make good sense, in spite of appearances to the contrary.

Many times it seems that there is not enough evidence in the associations of a single hour to warrant our being certain of the interpretation of a dream. This pessimistic impression often vanishes, if we are only persistent enough. Usually we will find that we are not making full use of evidence that is actually available. Instead of giving up to an indiscriminate skepticism, the interpreter should begin asking himself questions about details to which he has not yet paid adequate attention. Evidence is sometimes so abundant that its significance cannot be grasped all at once. In order to make full use of it, the interpreter must proceed as he would with a complicated jigsaw puzzle, trying to piece together first one part of it and then another, until finally he gets a glimpse of what the whole picture is like.

Examples. After this brief introduction, we can best describe our interpretive procedure by illustrating it. One example, based on an analysis of a case of melancholia by Helene Deutsch (1932), has already been published by one of the authors in *The Integration of Behavior* (1952).* In our

* Vol. I, Chap. 6.

next five chapters, we shall analyze four dreams and one day-dream. The first dream selected will illustrate the first major operation in our interpretive procedure—which is to understand the dream as a response to the immediate emotional situation of the dreamer at the time of dreaming. In our subsequent examples, we shall take account more and more of the great complexity of the dreamer's thought processes.

Every dream has many meanings. An important working assumption of our method is that the various meanings of a dream must fit *together* intelligibly as well as fitting intelligibly into the dreamer's emotional situation at the moment of dreaming. These two working hypotheses turn out to be our most rigorous check, indeed, our only adequate check on our interpretive procedure. We call this part of our interpretive procedure reconstructing the cognitive structure of the dream.

THEORETICAL IMPLICATIONS

The purpose of these essays is not primarily theoretical. Nevertheless, when we succeed in finding the sense that lies hidden in a dream, what we find often has important theoretical implications. In our next few chapters, we shall discuss such theoretical implications, one by one, as they emerge from each dream analysis.* We shall postpone further discussion of theory until Part Three of this work, when we shall try to piece together some of our theoretical insights into a comprehensive picture of the thought processes in dreaming.

* However, our theoretical conclusions are based, of course, on many dream analyses, not only on the few analyses reported in these pages.

A DREAM'S RESPONSE
TO EMOTIONAL SITUATION
AT TIME OF DREAMING

The patient from whose analysis the following excerpts are quoted was a thirty-four-year-old married man with four children who was being analyzed as an outpatient in a hospital. In order to understand the most obvious allusions in the dream that we have selected, it is necessary only to mention that his analyst, Dr. David Hamburg, was second in command of the hospital and had an office next to the office of the medical director. In the Army, some years previously, the patient had been a noncommissioned officer. We shall report first a dream reported in this patient's one hundredth analytic interview. Then we shall report the associations that followed during the rest of this hour. Later, we shall report parts of an earlier hour (98). Our excerpts are based on the analyst's notes, which were written down during the hour.

DREAM, HOUR 100.*

In the dream, I was in the Army again. Went into the mess-hall with another guy. Had a little trouble getting food [vague]. Then I saw a couple of guys I recognized. A Southerner called "the Colonel," actually a private, said: "Sit down. I'll take care of you. Will serve you like a king, on gold plates." I said: "Never mind the plates; just get good food."

Then this guy's appearance changed—he now looked like Jack Benny. He said he was Jack Benny's brother. I said, "Are you related?" Everybody laughed.

Then the scene changed. We were both being chased, going through a tunnel. I said, "This is ridiculous; if you are the brother of Jack Benny, who has millions, why doesn't he help you out?"

As in many dreams, the manifest content of this dream does not at first seem to make sense. The reason is probably that we do not know how it fits into the context of the patient's life. We should like, in particular, to know whether anything has happened recently to stimulate the patient to dream this dream. With this question in mind, we turn next to the patient's associations.

ASSOCIATIONS.

The remark about the brother reminds me that I feel as though I were unrelated to my own brothers. (In association to running through the tunnel, the patient repeats:) Why doesn't he help you out? (With a laugh, he

---

* Throughout, the patient's statements, when directly quoted, are set off, without quotation marks. When indirectly quoted, they are set off and enclosed in parentheses. Square brackets indicate the analyst's observations and comments.

says:) Maybe I have the idea that one brother should help another.

When I was in the Army, I was close to "the Colonel." "The Colonel" was willing to do quite a bit for me.

The gold plate business seemed odd to me. I don't care for a lot of bullshit, just the facts—don't flower it up. Sometimes people will give you a medal, then lay the egg.

[End of spontaneous associations.]

ANALYST: Any associations to the mess-hall?

PATIENT: Big mess-hall, few people in it.

ANALYST: Tell me about "the Colonel."

PATIENT: He came from Georgia. Had a lot of dogs. Went hunting on horseback. Sometimes I felt he was bull-shitting me. He was good-hearted, yet tight with money. I finally told him he'd have to share gas expenses for my car.

A number of statements he made didn't ring the bell [i.e., turned out to be not true].

He seemed to look up to me and follow me around like a puppy dog.

ANALYST: Jack Benny?

PATIENT: He has been around so long. Wonder what he's got. Doesn't seem to have much. Yet has made millions. I do appreciate his humor and enjoy him. [Long pause.]

I am thinking about "the Colonel" again. I was eager to get out of the Army. "The Colonel" re-enlisted. I have heard from him since the war a couple of times. I wrote last, then heard no more from him.

There was a lieutenant in the Medical Corps, a doctor, for whom "the Colonel" worked in the Army. Rough man. The lieutenant said I was goldbricking, using my dermatitis as an excuse for discharge. It wasn't so. The major, an overseas veteran, overruled the lieutenant and told him off; he got me discharged.

Thinking back, service years weren't bad. Rather enjoyed them. Liked freedom, evenings off, weekend passes.

(Analyst summarizes the manifest content of the dream: (1) pleasant setting; (2) nice attention; (3) in danger, those who could help, don't. Why dream about this now?)

PATIENT: [Laughs.] The dream is related to the analysis. I would like you to give me answers and tell me what to do.

ANALYST: You make your therapist very powerful. In an earlier dream, you depicted me as Mr. Eisenhower, now as Jack Benny. Isn't this expecting a lot—setting up for a likely disappointment? Does the "bullshit" perhaps refer to me?

PATIENT: When I thought I wasn't doing well, you said I was doing O.K. I thought maybe you were bullshitting to encourage me.

ANALYST: You perhaps are suspicious of attention, encouragement. The dream seems to say: "Attention leads to danger; powerful people don't help." Perhaps you want attention and importance, as in the dream, but find this dangerous.

PATIENT: In the dream, something nice is followed by danger. It's always this way. You must pay for pleasure. If someone does something nice for you, they'll want repayment.

As we read these associations, they still do not seem to make much sense. This may be due in part to the fact that we are reading only a report on paper. If we wish to make sense of this dream, our first task will be to use our empathic imagination to bring the dead record to life, to understand what the patient is saying as the human response of a live person.

Thus far, our intuition has not been able to get this kind of vivid empathy with the associations of this hour as a whole. So we look for some small part of the reported interview that might serve as a promising clue. As a possible clue, we select the following sentences from the manifest dream:

> A Southerner called "the Colonel," actually a private, said: "Sit down. I'll take care of you. Will serve you like a king, on gold plates." I said: "Never mind the plates; just get good food."

These sentences suggest a working hypothesis concerning the precipitating stimulus for this dream. Perhaps "the Colonel" is the analyst. Later in the hour, the patient confirms this suspicion. He says spontaneously, with a laugh, that the dream is related to the analysis. His laugh further betrays that he has some strong feelings about his relationship to the analyst. What are these feelings?

The sentences just quoted seem to have two implications. One is that the analyst is pretending to be more important than he actually is (a private who is called "Colonel"). The other is that he is trying to flatter the patient ("serve you like a king, gold plates"). The patient's associations about "the Colonel" and the "gold plate business" confirm these implications, especially the latter. In real life (in the Army), the patient was a sergeant. "The Colonel" was a private who "seemed to look up to the patient and follow him around like a puppy dog." The patient also repeats that he "didn't care for a lot of bullshit. Just the facts—don't flower it up." The next sentence even implies that the analyst's flattery is leading to something unpleasant: "Sometimes people give you a medal, then lay the egg."

All this suggests the hypothesis that the dream under discussion was a reaction to something that the analyst said, perhaps in the preceding hour (99). Before the end of the hour that we are now discussing (100), the patient spontaneously confirms this hypothesis by recalling something that the analyst had recently said to him: when the patient thought he was not doing well, the therapist said that he was doing O.K. The patient thought that maybe the therapist was "bullshitting" to encourage him.

Up to this point, we have been using our intuition imaginatively. Now we have reached a point where critical evaluation is indicated. The patient has recalled that the analyst told him that he was getting along all right. We have suspected that this may have been the precipitating stimulus for his dream. Appraising this suggestion critically, we now feel that the patient's need to repudiate the analyst's encouragement is excessive. What reason did the patient have to react so strongly to such a casual encouragement?

To check this point, we turn back to find out what the analyst did say. At the end of Hour 99, the patient had remarked that he had been "quite impressed" in the last hour (i.e., 98) when the analyst had told him that this was one of the "most important sessions we'd had." The patient "almost wasn't going to tell" the analyst, he adds. This statement had followed a long pause, during which the patient had grunted and seemed tense. (Up to this time, during the earlier part of the hour, he had been talking about seemingly unrelated matters.)

The patient's reluctance to tell the analyst and, still more, the long pause that preceded his doing so confirm our impression that the analyst's encouraging remarks had involved the patient in much more conflict than we should expect. So now we turn back to Hour 98 in order to find out what had been said. If possible, we should like to discover the nature of the conflict that had been stirred up in that session.

In the analyst's notes on Hour 98, we do not find the remark that the patient attributed to him. (The analyst had probably failed to note it.) We do learn, however, that in this hour a conflict of considerable intensity had been activated. With only a few omissions, we shall report the complete notes of this interview.

(The patient talks about a movie he saw Friday, *A Man Called Peter*. He was deeply moved by it. Death seems especially moving. The hero's wife reminded him of his wife. He felt an acute sense of appreciating his wife. He thought of how much he would miss her if she were to die.)

(The patient had tears in his eyes when telling her this. He found it very difficult to tell her. Almost gave it up.)

ANALYST: Why was it so hard?

PATIENT: I don't know. . . . Perhaps I feel that nobody wants to listen to it. . . . Also feel that these things are understood, but not expressed.

This is the first time I've felt it so deeply. I know she felt it too; I could feel her increased heartbeat. [Chuckles.]

Strange that I should feel so deeply moved. It's a new experience for me. [Scratching.] I was very glad I told her.

ANALYST: Why is it so difficult to express such feelings?

PATIENT: I am afraid of not being accepted, for example,

by Bertha (a girl whom he had loved before marriage).
Afraid I might stick my neck out and find that she didn't
care much for me. Hadn't intended to have intercourse,
but my telling her what I felt naturally led to it. [The
patient is now again talking about his wife.]

Will this feeling always be so intense? It seemed tre-
mendous, I had goose-pimples, etc.

ANALYST: It is a new experience for you. It will probably
become less intense as it becomes more familiar. Yet your
attitude seems to be that there's something wrong about
being emotionally excited.

[Long pause.] (Then the patient says he is going to
Riverview with his two older children tomorrow. He
speaks affectionately of his children.)

PATIENT: Seems like a long hour after telling you what
I had done. [His having felt great affection for his wife
and telling her so.]

It was hard to tell you. I thought you might think it
irrelevant or silly. Really childish or like a woman.

ANALYST: You are held back from expressing wishes for
affection, closeness, and tenderness by feeling that this
would be acting like a little child, infantile, or like a
woman, sissy, soft; in either case, a real weakness, something to be ashamed of. Also, as you brought out earlier
in the hour, there is a fear that you might be rejected. I
look on the expression of your feelings as natural and
healthy.

PATIENT: [At door, embarrassed.] It's like falling in
love all over again . . . maybe better than the first time.

Now we have found a conflict that is at least quantitatively
adequate to account for the patient's repudiating the analyst's

encouragement two hours later. Let us examine this conflict more carefully. It is a conscious one—one of intense embarrassment about admitting warm, appreciative, tender feelings toward his wife. Intuitively, we can sense that this patient's unusual reticence about betraying tender emotions may have a cultural background. Such reticence is much more usual in people with a Teutonic heritage, for example. Among some southern peoples, it is much more acceptable, for men as well as women, to give open expression to warm, tender emotions. Also, we should not lose sight of the possibility that, in this patient's case, there may be strong individual and personal reasons for his embarrassment about admitting tender feelings.

Now we encounter another puzzling fact. Whatever the reasons for this reaction, the patient's chagrin afterward was even more intense than his embarrassment during the hour. Before and during the hour, he had been able to tell first his wife and then the analyst about his tender feelings toward her. His very last remark in this hour is particularly impressive. "Like falling in love all over again . . . maybe better than the first time." In the next hour (99), he does not mention any of this until the end of the interview. Then, after a long, tense pause, he says that he had been "quite impressed" with the analyst's evaluation of the interview. He almost was not going to tell the analyst, he adds. In Hour 100, as we have seen, his negative reaction goes further. He accuses the analyst of "bullshitting" and remembers only that the analyst told him that he was getting along "O.K."

How do we account for the fact that his chagrin afterward was so much greater than his initial embarrassment? In order to answer this question, we look for clues in Hour 100. One fact of which we have not yet taken adequate account is that Dream 100 not only belittles the analyst's interpretation, but also betrays a strong urge to depreciate the analyst himself. One detail is particularly revealing: the man who represents the analyst was not only a private who let himself be called "Colonel"; but was also one who "seemed to look up to" the patient, to "follow him around like a puppy dog." Intuitively, it is easy to recognize the implication of this detail. It is an inverted picture of the patient's own intensely dependent affection for the analyst.

Once more we must ask: Is there any reason why his conflict about his affection for the analyst should have been more intense after Hour 98? Two more details give us the answer to this question. His last remark in Hour 98 reveals the fact that he was not only embarrassed, but also pleased and thrilled by the release of his tender feelings for his wife. It was "like falling in love all over again." At the end of the next hour (99), he admits that he was "quite impressed" with the analyst, too.

Now we can understand why his chagrin became so much more intense after Hour 98. His release of affection for his wife had been accompanied by an intensification of his admiring affection for the analyst. Then this welling up of affection had called forth a sharp reaction. His admiring affection had made the analyst great. In his dream (100), he must reverse his loving "overestimation" of the analyst by degrading him from a colonel to a private and accusing him of "bullshitting."

In our attempts at interpretive reasoning, as we have just illustrated, we start with the most promising clue that we can find. Then we proceed, utilizing one bit of evidence after another, to build up our picture of the patient's motivations.

Sometimes, after seemingly satisfactory progress, we encounter a block. We come on evidence that we are unable, at least for the moment, to reconcile with our hypotheses. Then we have to make a fresh start with other evidence and try anew.

At other times, after laboriously integrating one clue after another, we finally come to an understanding that accounts for many details of the material that we have not yet used in building our hypotheses. Such an opening-up of perspective on facts that we had not yet considered carefully gives us the essential confirmation that we hope for while we are still struggling with the initial task of reasoning carefully from more detailed evidence.

The authors believe that they have reached such a point in the interpretive effort in which they are now engaged. To check this impression, we shall examine two other episodes in the dream, which we have not yet studied carefully:

> In the dream, I was in the Army again. Went into the mess-hall with another guy. Had a little trouble getting food [vague]. Then I saw a couple of guys I recognized. A Southerner called "the Colonel," actually a private, said, "Sit down. I'll take care of you."
>
> Then this guy's appearance changed—he now looked like Jack Benny. He said he was Jack Benny's brother. I said, "Are you related?" Everybody laughed.

In the first episode, the patient is in the Army, rather than in the hospital, where he comes to see the analyst for his treatment. This substitution can easily be recognized as a defense against any feelings of tenderness or dependence. The Army is (officially) an impersonal world where any tenderness or sentimentality is out of place. In the mess-hall, the patient can expect to be fed as a matter of course but without any molly-coddling. ("Never mind the plates; Just get good food.") Instead of the analyst, whose "taking care" of him he so much appreciates (in spite of his reluctance to admit it), the dream has substituted a "Southerner called 'the Colonel.'" We have already discussed the implications of the fact that this man is only a private, though he is called "Colonel." The dream's choice of a Southerner is probably related to the graciousness and tenderness, especially toward women, that is part of the Southern ideal of a gentleman. To the patient, such behavior is soft in contrast to his own austere ideal of masculinity, which regards tender emotions as feminine or soft.

We turn now to the third dream episode. Jack Benny is a comedian whose words need not be taken seriously. This is in accord with the patient's need to make little of the analyst's encouragement and praise, which so pleased him. In the dream, the analyst is identified, not with Jack Benny, but with Jack Benny's brother. This is a reference to the psychiatrist who is head of the hospital. The patient's analyst is closely associated with this psychiatrist (Jack Benny) as second in command, with an office next to the chief's. In the dream, the patient debunks the analyst again with his question, "Are you related?"—which calls forth a laugh from everyone.

Turning to the last episode in the dream, we once more strike a block.

> Then the scene changed. We were both being chased, going through a tunnel. I said, "This is ridiculous; if you are the brother of Jack Benny, who has millions, why doesn't he help you out?"

It is not easy to see how being chased through a tunnel fits into the context of an intense need to repudiate tender emotions. Still, such a discrepancy is often a clue stimulating us to look for a more comprehensive insight.

Can we find any hints to suggest the links that may be missing? The last sentence in the dream seems to be getting back to the theme of debunking the analyst, in this case debunking the analyst's relation to his chief. Later in the hour, he comes around to the theme of discharge from the Army. The patient was eager to get out of the Army. "The Colonel," on the other hand, re-enlisted. A lieutenant countermanded the patient's application for discharge, said that the patient was using his dermatitis as "goldbricking"; but a major overruled the lieutenant, and the patient was discharged.

To the authors, the patient's talk about discharge from the Army suggests that he may be thinking about discharge from his treatment. Perhaps he has projected his own chagrin about the surge of loving feelings which he revealed to the analyst at the end of Hour 98. Now he is attributing his own shocked feelings to the hospital authorities. He and the analyst are both being chased out of the hospital. It is significant that they are both being chased, which implies that they were both involved in the "love scene" at the end of Hour 98. Although he did not say so, the patient was in love not only with his wife but also with the analyst. It is significant that he keeps the analyst with him in his fantasy of being discharged from treatment.

Can we be certain of this last bit of interpretation? This is a matter of intuitive judgment, since we can as yet find no further evidence to test it. It is probable that further evidence will come later that will serve as a further check on our interpretation of this dream. (We shall return to this question in Chapter VIII.)

FURTHER DISCUSSION OF
OUR INTERPRETIVE APPROACH

With the foregoing dream interpretation as a sample, we return to a summary and further discussion of our interpretive approach. As stated earlier, both phases of our interpretive procedure are intuitive. Both are based on the research analyst's empathic understanding of what the patient says and does. The essential difference between our objectively critical procedure and the more usual "direct-intuitive" approach is that the analyst's capacity for empathic understanding is used not only imaginatively but *also* as a basis for critical judgment.

There is still another difference. In our usual intuitive approach, we often assume that we are basing our interpretation on all the available evidence. When we interpret a dream, for example, we assume that the analyst's unconscious has taken account of all the details of the dream and of all the associations reported at the time. In our objectively critical approach, we do not make this assumption. We try rather to discover on just what evidence the analyst has based his intuitive inference. When we thus make the analyst's intuitive reasoning explicit, we often find that his interpretation has been suggested by only one small part of the evidence. (This is probably the most frequent reason why analysts do not always agree on the interpretation of a particular dream. In many cases, each analyst has based his interpretation on a different part of the evidence.) After all, the whole mass of evidence constituted by a dream and its associations is usually too

all interpretation involves a direct denial of
our therapeutic procedure. The disturbing
ories that are responsible for each patient's
conscious. After a long time (months or even
yst may succeed in bringing them back to the
ousness. In the meantime, he can only guess
hey are. More important for our present dis-
fact that the analyst must also either guess or
y to day, just what the motives that prevent the
ning conscious of his repressed wishes are. The
f does not know why he is resisting. The analyst
et the patient to recover repressed wishes and
ess he is able to infer what the motives for the
tances are. Then he must tell the patient about
or his resistance. From beginning to end, our
rocedure involves our ability to make correct into communicate them to the patient.

later, the authors believe, we must return to the
ve have been discussing in this chapter. We must
r a middle course between excessive faith in our
wers and a too-great skepticism. Instead of trying
our intuitive insights, we should set ourselves
checking our interpretive inferences, step by step,
eed.

l conclude this chapter with a warning: *An objec-*
cal approach to interpretation is an art that must

to convert his simple intuitive method into an ob-
critical one, an analyst must abandon his illusion
n grasp all the evidence at a single glance. It is also
gh to examine the evidence for and against a final

---

great to be grasped at a single glance, even by a very able
analyst.

Our objectively critical approach attempts to be more realistic about the analyst's limited capacity for intuitive understanding. We concentrate frankly on parts of the evidence,
one at a time, trying, at each point, to select just that part of
the evidence the significance of which we are surest that we
can grasp (intuitively). Then, step by step, we try to integrate
our partial insights until we can build up a trustworthy understanding of the whole.

Of course, we never succeed in understanding everything.
An essential feature of our method is that we train ourselves
to be sensitive to gaps and discrepancies in the evidence so
that, when we find a discrepancy, we try to discover the reason
for it. Actually, gaps and discrepancies in the evidence are
our *best clues* for discovering relationships that we had not yet
suspected. For example, in the dream analysis just reported,
we realized that the analyst's telling the patient that he was
getting along "O.K." was not a stimulus sufficient to account
for the patient's strong need to repudiate the analyst's encouragement. This led us to look back to the preceding interviews until we found evidence of the patient's conflict about
expressing tender feelings for his wife. Then we found another
discrepancy—the fact that his chagrin after Hour 98 had been
much greater than his embarrassment during the hour. Thus
challenged, we re-examined the dream and associations in
Hour 100. We discovered that the patient had an even greater
conflict about betraying his affectionate, but repressed, feelings toward the analyst than about expressing his tender feelings toward his wife.

A carefully cultivated sensitivity to gaps and discrepancies
is our best antidote against an uncritical tendency to which,

as "intuitive" analysts, we are often prone. The interpretive "bad habits" to which we refer might be called a "Procrustean bed" technique. Starting with an interpretation based on only part of the evidence, we proceed next to force the rest of the material to fit our first impression. In the more carefully checked procedure that we are now describing, we are most often tempted to do this at the point when our hypotheses finally seem to open up a new perspective, accounting for facts that we had not yet considered carefully. Such a new perspective may be the long-awaited confirmation of the work we have done so far. Yet we must be on our guard against forcing the evidence into a preconceived pattern. We know of no way to avoid this, except by training ourselves to be sensitive to gaps and discrepancies in our evidence.

We know that many analysts will be impatient of all this painstaking effort devoted to the elucidation of one dream. "Has not our usual intuitive approach served us well in the past?" they may say. "We already have a rough intuitive check on our interpretations. If we miss some nuances in our interpretations today, sooner or later the patient's associative material will bring them out more clearly."

Unfortunately, this is often a false hope.

There is an understandable emotional reason for such impatient protests. A sudden flash of insight is a highly satisfying experience. In order to submit the new insight to a painstaking process of checking, we must interrupt this thrill of omniscient satisfaction.

Yet, the result is often worth it. The new perspective that can sometimes be won is well worth the painstaking effort that made it possible.

Our technique of systematic critical evaluation of inter-

pretations may h
pathology. Somet
men will suffice fo
must judiciously s
and examined und
painstaking effort
to understand the t

The attitudes of
strangely paradoxic
have nothing more t
cidated the process o
in the transference, th
At other times, we g
with the problem of u
a psychoanalytic treat
nothing about the thera
extensive projects for co
data. Then we discover
it has become more, rathe

Our reaction formatio
much psychoanalytic inte
From a too-naïve faith i
treme skepticism in which
terpretations that go beyon
data. Lurking in the backg
that our data should not i
should speak for themselve
choanalysis has so often bee
vindicate our science by me
and avoiding all inference.

In order to rid ourselves
to remind ourselves why we

hope of avoiding
the rationale of
wishes and men
neurosis are un
years), the ana
patient's consci
or infer what
cussion is the
infer, from da
patient's becor
patient himsel
cannot ever g
memories unl
patient's resis
the motives
therapeutic p
ferences and

Sooner or
task which
learn to ste
intuitive po
to renounce
the task of
as we proc

We sha
tively crit
be learned
In orde
jectively
that he ca
not enou

great to be grasped at a single glance, even by a very able analyst.

Our objectively critical approach attempts to be more realistic about the analyst's limited capacity for intuitive understanding. We concentrate frankly on parts of the evidence, one at a time, trying, at each point, to select just that part of the evidence the significance of which we are surest that we can grasp (intuitively). Then, step by step, we try to integrate our partial insights until we can build up a trustworthy understanding of the whole.

Of course, we never succeed in understanding everything. An essential feature of our method is that we train ourselves to be sensitive to gaps and discrepancies in the evidence so that, when we find a discrepancy, we try to discover the reason for it. Actually, gaps and discrepancies in the evidence are our *best clues* for discovering relationships that we had not yet suspected. For example, in the dream analysis just reported, we realized that the analyst's telling the patient that he was getting along "O.K." was not a stimulus sufficient to account for the patient's strong need to repudiate the analyst's encouragement. This led us to look back to the preceding interviews until we found evidence of the patient's conflict about expressing tender feelings for his wife. Then we found another discrepancy—the fact that his chagrin after Hour 98 had been much greater than his embarrassment during the hour. Thus challenged, we re-examined the dream and associations in Hour 100. We discovered that the patient had an even greater conflict about betraying his affectionate, but repressed, feelings toward the analyst than about expressing his tender feelings toward his wife.

A carefully cultivated sensitivity to gaps and discrepancies is our best antidote against an uncritical tendency to which, as "intuitive" analysts, we are often prone. The interpretive "bad habits" to which we refer might be called a "Procrustean bed" technique. Starting with an interpretation based on only part of the evidence, we proceed next to force the rest of the material to fit our first impression. In the more carefully checked procedure that we are now describing, we are most often tempted to do this at the point when our hypotheses finally seem to open up a new perspective, accounting for facts that we had not yet considered carefully. Such a new perspective may be the long-awaited confirmation of the work we have done so far. Yet we must be on our guard against forcing the evidence into a preconceived pattern. We know of no way to avoid this, except by training ourselves to be sensitive to gaps and discrepancies in our evidence.

We know that many analysts will be impatient of all this painstaking effort devoted to the elucidation of one dream. "Has not our usual intuitive approach served us well in the past?" they may say. "We already have a rough intuitive check on our interpretations. If we miss some nuances in our interpretations today, sooner or later the patient's associative material will bring them out more clearly."

Unfortunately, this is often a false hope.

There is an understandable emotional reason for such impatient protests. A sudden flash of insight is a highly satisfying experience. In order to submit the new insight to a painstaking process of checking, we must interrupt this thrill of omniscient satisfaction.

Yet, the result is often worth it. The new perspective that can sometimes be won is well worth the painstaking effort that made it possible.

Our technique of systematic critical evaluation of interpretations may be compared to the use of a microscope in pathology. Sometimes careful examination of a gross specimen will suffice for a diagnosis; at other times, the pathologist must judiciously select certain areas to be cut up in sections and examined under the microscope. The rewards for such painstaking effort are particularly great when we are trying to understand the therapeutic process.

The attitudes of analysts toward therapeutic research are strangely paradoxical. Some analysts seem to feel that we have nothing more to learn. Since Freud has beautifully elucidated the process of working through an infantile neurosis in the transference, this is all that we need to know, we think. At other times, we go to the opposite extreme. When faced with the problem of understanding the day-to-day course of a psychoanalytic treatment, we sometimes feel that we know nothing about the therapeutic process. In this mood, we plan extensive projects for collecting and recording more and more data. Then we discover that our data are so voluminous that it has become more, rather than less, difficult to interpret them.

Our reaction formation against the uncritical character of much psychoanalytic interpretation often takes another form. From a too-naïve faith in our intuitions, we turn to an extreme skepticism in which we distrust all inferences and interpretations that go beyond a mere summarizing of observed data. Lurking in the background is a hope, to which we cling, that our data should not need to be interpreted. The data should speak for themselves. The scientific validity of psychoanalysis has so often been doubted that we would like to vindicate our science by merely reporting our observations and avoiding all inference.

In order to rid ourselves of this seductive hope, it is well to remind ourselves why we know that it is a vain one. The hope of avoiding all interpretation involves a direct denial of the rationale of our therapeutic procedure. The disturbing wishes and memories that are responsible for each patient's neurosis are unconscious. After a long time (months or even years), the analyst may succeed in bringing them back to the patient's consciousness. In the meantime, he can only guess or infer what they are. More important for our present discussion is the fact that the analyst must also either guess or infer, from day to day, just what the motives that prevent the patient's becoming conscious of his repressed wishes are. The patient himself does not know why he is resisting. The analyst cannot ever get the patient to recover repressed wishes and memories unless he is able to infer what the motives for the patient's resistances are. Then he must tell the patient about the motives for his resistance. From beginning to end, our therapeutic procedure involves our ability to make correct inferences and to communicate them to the patient.

Sooner or later, the authors believe, we must return to the task which we have been discussing in this chapter. We must learn to steer a middle course between excessive faith in our intuitive powers and a too-great skepticism. Instead of trying to renounce our intuitive insights, we should set ourselves the task of checking our interpretive inferences, step by step, as we proceed.

We shall conclude this chapter with a warning: *An objectively critical approach to interpretation is an art that must be learned.*

In order to convert his simple intuitive method into an objectively critical one, an analyst must abandon his illusion that he can grasp all the evidence at a single glance. It is also not enough to examine the evidence for and against a final